Dear Parent:

Congratulations! Your child is taking the first steps on an exciting journey. The destination? Independent reading!

STEP INTO READING® will help your child get there. The program offers five steps to reading success. Each step includes fun stories and colorful art. There are also Step into Reading Sticker Books, Step into Reading Math Readers, Step into Reading Write-In Readers, Step into Reading Phonics Readers, and Step into Reading Phonics First Steps! Boxed Sets—a complete literacy program with something for every child.

Learning to Read, Step by Step!

Ready to Read   Preschool–Kindergarten
• big type and easy words • rhyme and rhythm • picture clues
For children who know the alphabet and are eager to begin reading.

Reading with Help   Preschool–Grade 1
• basic vocabulary • short sentences • simple stories
For children who recognize familiar words and sound out new words with help.

Reading on Your Own   Grades 1–3
• engaging characters • easy-to-follow plots • popular topics
For children who are ready to read on their own.

Reading Paragraphs   Grades 2–3
• challenging vocabulary • short paragraphs • exciting stories
For newly independent readers who read simple sentences with confidence.

Ready for Chapters   Grades 2–4
• chapters • longer paragraphs • full-color art
For children who want to take the plunge into chapter books but still like colorful pictures.

STEP INTO READING® is designed to give every child a successful reading experience. The grade levels are only guides. Children can progress through the steps at their own speed, developing confidence in their reading, no matter what their grade.

Remember, a lifetime love of reading starts with a single step!

The authors and editor would like to thank Dr. Michael Brett-Surman, Museum Specialist for Dinosaurs at the National Museum of Natural History of the Smithsonian Institution, for his assistance in the preparation of this book.

To my loving parents, Jack and Betty Chin, and my dear husband, Jeff. —Karen Chin

To Anne, for inspiration. —Thom Holmes

Dedicated with great love and admiration to my mentor and friend, Dr. Louis Jacobs, who made all this possible! —Karen Carr

PHOTO CREDITS: © Louis Psihoyos/psihoyos.com, p. 4; courtesy Dr. Karen Chin, p. 23 and p. 45; © SEPM (Society for Sedimentary Geology), coprolite specimen courtesy of the Royal Tyrrell Museum/Alberta Community Development, p. 42.

www.stepintoreading.com
www.jpinstitute.com

Educators and librarians, for a variety of teaching tools, visit us at www.randomhouse.com/teachers

Library of Congress Cataloging-in-Publication Data
Chin, Karen.
Dino dung : the scoop on fossil feces / by Karen Chin and Thom Holmes ; illustrated by Karen Carr. — 1st ed.
    p. cm. — (Step into reading. Step 5)
ISBN 0-375-82702-1 (trade) — ISBN 0-375-92702-6 (lib. bdg.)
1. Coprolites—Juvenile literature. 2. Dinosaurs—Food—Juvenile literature. I. Holmes, Thom. II. Carr, Karen, 1960–. III. Title. IV. Series.
QE899.2.C67C48 2004
567.9—dc22
2004000287

Printed in the United States of America First Edition 10 9 8 7 6 5 4 3 2 1

A Note to Parents: This book is appropriate for ages 7 and up. The *Jurassic Park* films are rated PG-13. Consult www.filmratings.com for further information.

JURASSIC PARK INSTITUTE

DINO DUNG

The Scoop on Fossil Feces

by Dr. Karen Chin and Thom Holmes
illustrated by Karen Carr

Random House New York

Dr. Karen Chin surrounded by coprolites—and some coprolite look-alikes!

Introduction

Studying prehistoric animals is like looking at a jigsaw puzzle that is missing many pieces. How do we know what the finished picture should look like? Scientists use fossils to help fill in the missing image.

My name is Karen Chin and I am a paleontologist (PAY-lee-un-TOL-uh-jist). My job is to study fossils and figure out the puzzle of prehistoric life. It's great fun, and I often feel like a detective.

When you think of fossils, you may think of bones and shells. But I examine something else that dinosaurs and prehistoric animals left behind. I study fossil feces (FEE-seez)!

I'm going to tell you about ancient dung and what we can learn from it. But first, you should know that the science of fossil feces has a history as old as the science of dinosaurs.

Chapter 1
The Case of the Weird White Blobs

Imagine this. It is the early 1820s, and you are looking for fossils in a dark cave in England. As you dig, you find bones of ancient hyenas (hie-EE-nuhz), elephants, and hippopotami (hip-uh-POT-uh-my).

Among the fossil bones, you also find some white rocklike blobs about the size of a cherry. What could they be? They are

definitely not bones. Can they be fossils as well?

That is what geologist William Buckland wondered. He was the scientist who explored that cave in England. The little white blobs fascinated him. First, he looked for clues in the cave. The bones he found suggested that ancient hyenas had eaten other animals in the cave. If that was true, the white blobs might be the result of those feasts.

Buckland had an idea. Maybe he had discovered fossilized feces!

How could Buckland figure out if he'd really discovered prehistoric feces? Nobody had ever claimed such a thing before.

William Buckland was a good scientist who tested his theories. He went to the zoo and examined the feces of living hyenas. This probably seemed like a very odd thing to do! But what he found helped clear up the mystery.

First, he compared the shape of the ancient blobs to hyena feces. They were indeed similar. Next, with the help of a fellow scientist, he compared the minerals found in the blobs with those found in fresh feces. Bingo! They were so much alike that it left little doubt—Buckland's idea was correct! He was the first scientist to identify fossilized feces.

The first *dinosaur* would not be named until almost 20 years later, in 1842!

Buckland also became famous as an expert on dinosaurs. But he never lost his interest in fossil feces. He even came up with the scientific name for fossil dung. *Coprolite* (KOP-ruh-lite) means "dung stone." It combines the Greek words *kopros* (dung) and *lithos* (stone).

Buckland was a great scientific detective. He knew that clues to the past could be found in the modern world. Paleontologists today do the same kind of detective work.

Discovering coprolites made Buckland a scientific pioneer, but there is still a lot to learn about fossil feces. Studying coprolites is a regular (pardon the pun!) "Who dung it" mystery!

Chapter 2
Left Behind

Fossils are evidence of ancient life preserved in rock. There are two basic kinds of fossils. When you see a dinosaur bone in a museum, you are looking at a *body* fossil. A body fossil preserves the bodily remains of an extinct animal. Bones, shells, and teeth are examples of body fossils.

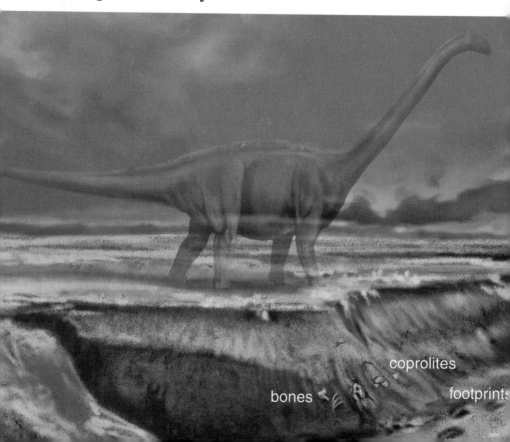

coprolites

bones

footprints

Another type of fossil is a *trace* fossil. Trace fossils preserve evidence of the activity of ancient animals. They are not part of the animal itself. Fossil footprints, burrows, and coprolites are all examples of trace fossils.

Body fossils tell us about the size and shape of extinct animals. Trace fossils tell us how animals behaved. For example, fossilized tracks and burrows can tell us how extinct animals moved and where they lived. But what in the world can we learn from old feces?

Chapter 3
From Food to Feces

All animals must eat food to live. After an animal eats, its digestive system goes to work. The body produces chemicals to break food down. Animals even have bacteria (tiny single-celled microorganisms) living inside their guts to help digest food. The digestive

system extracts as much energy as possible from the food.

But most animals can't digest everything they eat. Food that the body can't digest must be unloaded. Undigested food and old bacteria are packed up in the large intestine and ejected from the body. This waste is called feces, or fecal matter. The body seems to be saying, "We've finished with this batch of food. Next, please!"

We all know that fresh feces have an unpleasant smell. The odor is caused by stinky compounds that are by-products of digestion. We avoid feces because of the smell. This is a good reaction to have because fecal matter can sometimes spread disease.

But dung provides wonderful food for some creatures. Dung beetles would probably turn up their noses (if they *had* noses) at ice cream. But give them a pile of yummy dung and they're a happy bunch. Bacteria and fungi (FUN-guy) gobble up what the dung-eating animals leave behind.

So dung isn't bad stuff. It's actually a very important part of the process of living. It reminds us that nature constantly recycles waste. And that's a very good thing! If recycling didn't take place, we'd be up to our eyeballs in dung and other organic matter!

Why do scientists study feces? Remember that animals don't digest everything they eat. So dung usually contains bits and pieces of undigested food. Wildlife biologists study fresh animal feces, or scat, to learn what animals eat. This tells us a lot about how an animal lives as part of its ecosystem, the natural environment in which plants, animals, and microorganisms live together. It also explains why paleontologists study fossilized feces.

Of course, there's a huge difference between fresh scat and fossilized feces. Coprolites are really old! What makes them last so long?

Chapter 4
The Scat with Nine Lives

Bones are tough and hard. They can survive long after an animal dies. It is easy to see how bones can become fossils. But how does a soft pile of feces get preserved? Fresh dung usually doesn't last very long before it is broken down by weather, animals, or microorganisms. It takes very special circumstances to fossilize feces.

Feces are usually preserved in one of two ways. If left in a dry place, like a cave, feces can last thousands of years. Scientists have found coprolites from woolly mammoths and ancient humans that almost look fresh.

Dried feces in a cave.

Feces can last even longer—many millions of years—if they are turned to stone, or lithified (LITH-uh-fide). Feces must be buried under just the right conditions to be lithified. Buried feces are protected from rain and animals that might eat or trample them. Then, if the conditions are just right, the feces turn to stone.

Turning feces into stone may seem like magic. But scientists have learned that bacteria actually *help* lithify fossils. Of course, the bacteria don't *try* to preserve fossils. They don't even think! But as bacteria live, they change the chemistry around them. This helps minerals form. So the bacteria in feces may cause the fecal matter to become fossilized.

In most cases, feces have to be buried to be preserved.

Remember that feces can only become fossils if the conditions are perfect. This is why coprolites are usually less common than fossil bones. Think about it. A fossil bone comes from an animal that died long ago. How many times does an animal die in its lifetime? Only once. But how many times does an animal defecate in its lifetime? If feces were easily fossilized, coprolites would be lying all over the place!

Chapter 5
Is That What I Think It Is?

Coprolites come in all shapes and sizes. They can be as large as basketballs or as tiny as sesame seeds. Would you recognize a coprolite if you saw one? What clues would you look for?

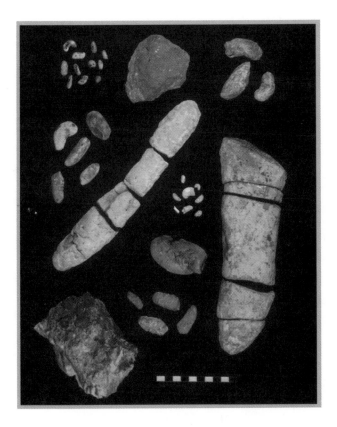

The most obvious clue is shape. Does the object in question resemble a deer pellet, a dog dropping, or a cow pie? Dried coprolites can look just like recent scat. They are still rather soft. Small lithified coprolites can also have the shape of fresh animal droppings. But when you pick them up, you realize that they are rock-hard.

Although shape can be telling, it is not always the best way to recognize a coprolite. Some rocks can fool you. They look a lot like fossil feces even though they are not. And some coprolites are so squashed and distorted that they don't look like droppings at all. Imagine what would happen if a herd of dinosaurs trampled a pile of fresh dung! As coprolites, they simply look like unusual rocks.

Another way to tell a coprolite from an ordinary rock is by what's inside. A rock that contains a lot of chopped-up bone or plant material might be fossil feces. But content—like shape—is not a foolproof test. Some rocks contain lots of shell or plant material even though they are not coprolites. So more clues are needed.

Remember William Buckland, who discovered the first coprolite? He figured out another way to tell a plain rock from a coprolite. He compared the chemical makeup of a rock to that of fresh feces. We know that the diets of carnivores (KAR-nuh-vorz), or meat-eaters, contain phosphorus (FAHS-fur-us). Therefore, phosphorus is also found in their feces. A coprolite left behind by a carnivore will contain more phosphorus than an ordinary rock. Not all coprolites were left by meat-eaters, but this is a good test for many fossil feces.

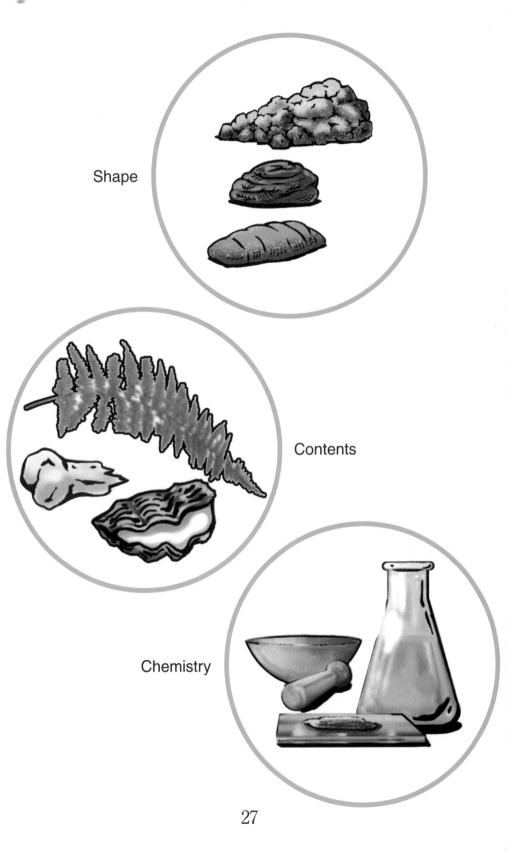

Shape

Contents

Chemistry

What color is a coprolite? You might think that they would all be brown, like fresh feces. But coprolite color can be as varied as coprolite shape. The process of lithification can turn coprolites a rainbow of colors. They might be orange, white, brown, gray, black, green, or even blue!

Like all good detectives, paleontologists examine many clues to figure out if a rock is a coprolite. The best clues are shape, contents, and chemical makeup.

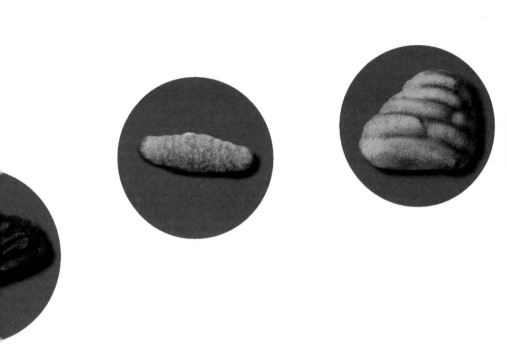

Chapter 6
Dung Detectives

Wildlife biologists can break open recent scat to see what's inside. But studying rock-hard coprolites is quite a different story. The good news is that they don't smell like fresh feces! So how do scientists study coprolites that are solid rock?

Paleontologists first look at the outside of a coprolite with a magnifying glass or microscope. Sometimes pieces of bone or other bits of ancient food can be seen sticking out of the surface. But sometimes the outside of a coprolite doesn't tell much at all. The best clues may be inside the coprolite.

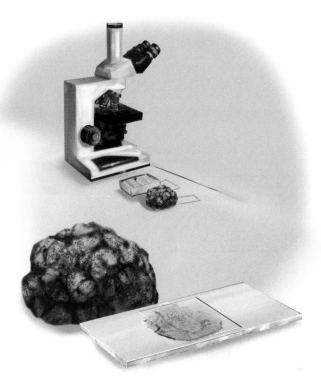

Fortunately, there are special saws that can cut into rock. Before cutting, scientists first carefully photograph the coprolite with a ruler next to it. This will remind them what it looked like and what size it was when it was whole. Then they cut off a very small slice with a rock saw. This slice is mounted on a glass slide and ground very thin so it can be examined under a microscope. This is done carefully so the whole coprolite isn't destroyed.

Chapter 7
Stories Feces Tell

Paleontologists study coprolites to learn about ancient ecosystems. Fossil feces can tell us things about the animals that were eaten and the animal that did the eating.

The Eaten:

The inside of a coprolite might tell you what an animal ate and how well it digested its food. If most of the food was digested, the inside of the coprolite may just look like uninteresting mineral mush. But when food residues are present, they can be quite beautiful under a microscope.

Some food residues have unusual shapes with distinctive patterns. Pretty as they may be, it is often difficult to tell what kind of food they once were. To solve this mystery, paleontologists often do as William Buckland did. They look at living organisms for clues. I look at the structure of plants and animals under a microscope. This helps me recognize the same kinds of structures in coprolites. Coprolites can have bone, shell, wood, or leaves in them. These body fossils help us identify the food that was eaten.

The Eater:

The most difficult part of studying fossil feces is trying to figure out who produced the feces. In other words . . . "Who dung it?"

This is so difficult to find out that in most cases we will never know. But there are many clues that can narrow down the list of suspects. One of the most important things to learn about a coprolite is its geological age. That is the time in the history of the earth when the feces were produced.

How old is *old*? Fossil feces may date back thousands or even millions of years. Dried coprolites are usually only thousands of years old. But some lithified coprolites were produced as many as 400 million years ago. Paleontologists figure this out by dating the age of the rock in which a coprolite is found.

Many kinds of animals have come and gone in the last 400 million years. The first dinosaurs appeared about 225 million years ago, but most of the dinosaurs (except for birds) died out 65 million years ago. The age of mammals came after that. The trick is knowing what kinds of animals were around when a coprolite was left behind. For example, since *T. rex* became extinct 65 million years ago, it could not have made a coprolite that is only 40 million years old.

In most cases, we will never know who dung it!

The next step is to look inside the coprolite for more clues. If you find the remains of undigested plants, you are holding the ancient dung of an herbivore (ER-buh-vor), or plant-eater. If the coprolite contains bits of bone or shell, it was left behind by a meat-eating carnivore. Knowing which plant-eaters and meat-eaters were around when the coprolite was left behind narrows the list of possible suspects.

Coprolite size provides another important clue to the dung-maker. But the size of a fecal pile can sometimes fool you. We know that a small animal can't produce a huge dung heap. But a large animal might very well make small feces. Can you think of an example? Hint: There's one with a long neck that lives in Africa. This tallest of animals produces a pile of grape-sized fecal pellets. (Answer: A giraffe!)

And remember that a fecal mass could have been squashed while it was still fresh.

Or it could have crumbled into smaller pieces after it was fossilized. It can be hard to tell how big the original pile was.

Chapter 8
The Mystery of the Dung Burrowers

One important collection of coprolites was found in the badlands of Montana. At first, these coprolites looked like ordinary gray rocks. But careful inspection showed that they were jam-packed with plant material. The age of the rocks in which the coprolites were found tells us that they are about 75 million years old. This was during a time called the Cretaceous (krih-TAY-shus) Period, when dinosaurs ruled the earth.

These coprolites were filled with bits of wood from a cone-bearing tree, like a redwood. This discovery was exciting because fossil feces from plant-eaters are rarely found. Some of the coprolites are nearly whole. The largest is about the size of a basketball!

In this particular case, there are several clues as to who left the feces. The size and contents tell us that a large plant-eater produced them. We also know that lots of bones from the herbivorous duckbilled dinosaur *Maiasaura* were found in the same rocks. These clues suggest that *Maiasaura* dinosaurs made these coprolites.

Big heaps of dinosaur dung would certainly have attracted insects. Burrows in the

Montana coprolites show that ancient critters once crawled in and around the dung. The burrows are so distinctive that we know they were produced by dung beetles.

These burrowed coprolites show how dinosaurs, trees, and dung beetles were linked in a Cretaceous ecosystem. The many burrows tell us that these ancient dung heaps were busy places. It would have taken a lot of work to recycle the zillions of tons of feces that the dinosaurs produced!

Chapter 9
The Case of the
Telltale Tyrannosaur

There is still much to learn from coprolites. Modern scientists use fancier equipment than Buckland did to study fossil feces. But we still use the same investigative methods to learn about the past. Here's a modern-day coprolite mystery.

Imagine this. It is the late 1990s, and someone has found what they think is a coprolite in the badlands of Alberta, Canada. Is it a coprolite? And if so, what does it tell us about ancient life?

My job is to answer these questions. The presence of phosphorus and chopped-up organic bits in the rock tell me this is indeed a coprolite. But are there enough clues to tell us what kind of animal left it behind?

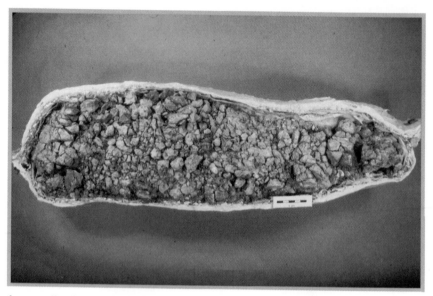
A coprolite from a large meat-eating dinosaur. It's about two feet long!

The rocks surrounding the coprolite are about 75 million years old. And the coprolite is a whopping two feet long! It is also filled with bits of chopped-up bones. These clues tell us that the "eater" was a huge carnivore that lived when dinosaurs roamed the earth.

This evidence points to one very suspicious culprit. The dung in question was probably made by a geologically older cousin of *Tyrannosaurus rex*. This tyrannosaur wasn't as large as *T. rex*, but it was certainly a fearsome dinosaur.

It's exciting to find a coprolite from a large meat-eating dinosaur. But this coprolite holds a few more surprises.

When I examine pieces from the large coprolite under a microscope, I see weird impressions. I compare them with modern plant and animal cells. After thinking about this for a long time, I figure out what these impressions might be. They look like fossilized muscle cells!

Like Buckland, I consult with other scientists. One is a medical doctor who studies fresh muscle cells. The people on our scientific team all agree. When these feces turned to rock, the shape of the victim's muscle cells was preserved. It's meat that had not been fully digested!

Finding traces of meat in a coprolite is a big surprise. How could this have happened? First, the tyrannosaur had not digested its meal very well. Then the feces were preserved quickly, so the meat didn't rot away.

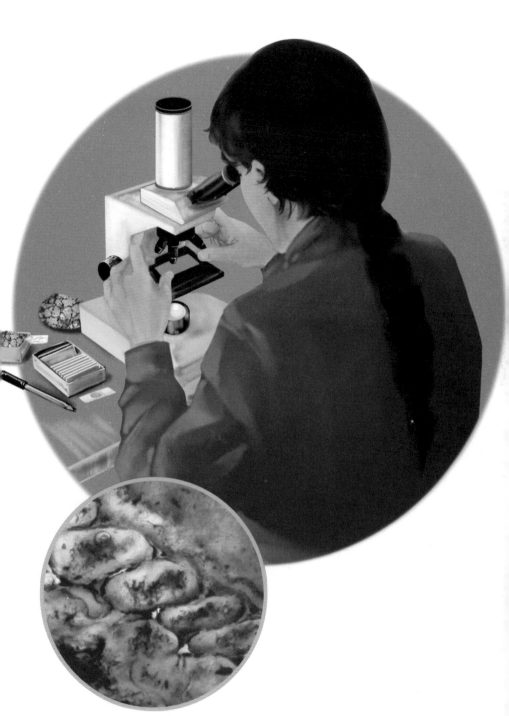

Fossilized muscle cells from undigested meat.

Chapter 10
Conclusion: It All Comes Out in the End

Now you see how the study of coprolites can lead to great discoveries about prehistoric life. Fossilized dung tells a story that bones cannot tell by themselves. The fossil feces tell

us about the food that prehistoric animals ate. And they tell us which plants and animals lived together in the ancient past.

Paleontologists rely on many skills to understand coprolites. They start with good fossil evidence and knowledge about living creatures. But it takes the skills of a detective and a great imagination to solve the puzzle of prehistoric life.

Life of a Fossil Feces Hunter

When Karen Chin was growing up, she was mostly interested in learning about *living* things. She loved the great outdoors and became a park ranger in Yellowstone and Glacier national parks. Many large mammals live in those parks, and when Chin took visitors on nature walks, she didn't always see the animals. She became good at looking for their traces, including scat. She showed people how to tell moose dung from elk dung.

Chin got interested in paleontology in college. Famed dinosaur expert Jack Horner put her to work preparing bones in his lab. The mystery of fossils fascinated her and she was hooked.